What, How, When, Where and Why

50 Answers

Marco Antonio Meza-Flores

What, how, when, where and why. 50 Answers.

First Edition (Canah editorial, 2014). Contact reverendo_czy@hotmail.com and grupocanah@gmail.com

Translator: José Antonio Alva Salas

Cover design: Job González Morejón

ISBN-13: 978-1503161719
ISBN-10: 1503161714

To my sons, Isaac and Gadiel, who have taught me so much over the years and have made me respond in the best way...Investigating.
I love them.

GRATITUDE

You cannot write a book without saying THANKS. Who to thank? I thank all those who have allowed me to walk with them and learn from them.

I want to make clear that God is wonderful to me, first, for giving me life, and then, for letting I share it with my beloved companions, thank you God.

Thanks to Mayra for the wonderful trip she has let me take with her, two wonderful children, Isaac and Gadiel, who have made me read more than I already did and for all the joy they add to my happiness.

Thanks to David N. Campos, without him, this book would have never been made, thanks brother, thanks for being you, for always being in the right place.

Thanks to CANAH, my dream and my alchemy, it is for Canah that I keep walking by places I would have never imagined.

And especially thanks to all my readers, simply for reading me. Happy journey!

INTRODUCTION

When I started writing this text it was great, I remember that was with David (my editor) in my office talking about many things and questions arose, some which many times arise randomly and others that we may not answer by the fear of not having answers.

Then I began the adventure of answering many things I've been asked in interviews, at conferences, in cells, everywhere; and shaped them, it was kind of a trip where I found life balms.

Fifty Answers is a practical, simple and full-of-answers handbook, the scholar background I have helped me solve many questions that are "headaches" and are then laid aside.

In this booklet you will find five basic questions of journalism: What, how, when, where and why; and with them, questions about life, happiness, peace, essence, dreams, God, religion, sex, being human and family.

We go deep into questions that seem simple for some, but that are very complex for others, and we give simple, yet, profound definitions (we settle them) to find what many look for...Answers.

Rev. Marco Antonio Meza-Flores
GJ Clinical Psychologist and Theologian

LIFE

WHAT IS LIFE?

You're born, grow, reproduce and die.

Throughout this process, we believe that life is limited to these principles, however, is not so simple, you cannot take a tree and try to stretch it for it to grow faster. In the same way you cannot force it to drop its seed before its time.

To understand what life is, we have to start by defining what life is, and that, within it, all that surrounds us is a symbol, and this symbol has a particular meaning; because even if something does not mean anything to me, that doesn't mean it does not issue a message.

Life is not just finishing a cycle stipulated by biology; if that were the case, all animals, plants, and humans beings would be the same, but, what distinguishes me from other living things?

I HAVE the ability to create and destroy. When have you heard a bird say "this time I will build a two-story nest" or a lioness say "enough, I'll be a

11

vegetarian"? Imagine an elephant say "starting today, I will diet" or a rabbit who thinks "from now on I will have sex only on Fridays and I'll use protection to avoid having such a numerous family". When have you seen an owl going through sleepless nights writing stories to leave a legacy to posterity?

Of course not, animals do not have the ability to decide, they act through instinct while we go by drive, needs. That makes us different, WE DECIDE.

So, what is life?

Life is the ability to make a decision if we want to create or destroy. Consequently, we can define "LIFE" as "CREATING".

How SHOULD WE LIVE?

AS YOU WANT

We are full of institutionalized phrases, instructions, directions and rules that, although some help us coexist, they also greatly overwhelm the creator of each intrivitrio.[1] The social contract is made for us to live within the politically correct parameters.

---

[1] This term will be explained below. Author Note.

A girl in a short skirt can't go out without a macho telling or doing something to her; and if this actually happens, we tend to blame the victim. If a woman breastfeeds in public, we do not know how to react. If a child goes naked or in underwear to a store, we laugh at him, mockingly, there are many examples. Every single one of them is shaped by what we call "social contract".

Amid all that, how should we live? Creating our own space, without trampling others and sharing the space with whoever wants to share it.

Previously we discussed that life begins from the decision to believe and create, not to be mediocre and thus, destroy.

It is very easy to destroy, it is part of what we are taught through competing against others, forgetting that the only competition worth is the one we have against ourselves; with so much noise, competition is part of the system and that who doesn't compete is named "weird".

Therefore, the best way to live is being yourself, not forgetting that you live with others, creating healthy spaces, clean from institutions and masks that overshadow you or others. A space of your own.

WHEN DOES LIFE BEGIN?
TODAY, HERE AND NOW

Usually we want to begin life "tomorrow" when there aren't as many problems, when my financial needs have been solved, when I have resolved this setback or the other. Wrong. Life starts today, here and now.

When you ask yourself when, you inevitably think of time, but time is a human invention to lock yourself into something nonexistent, again, you only have a moment, and that moment is here and now. The moment is you. You are your time.

People are educated to live "to have a better future", but that's absurd, you cannot have something that is not tangible, some use the past as a sofa and they suffer, "why am I doing so bad" or "I was better before", but the idea of being your own time is that we can break your schemes, your prejudice and your whole being.

Now, we do not talk about irresponsibility, it is adult-like to be responsible with the choices we make, consistency has to do with the decisions and actions, coherence, with what we were taught, and sometimes what we were taught is wrong, it is not ours, it does not fit us, and it is a burden.

When then? It must be today. Today is the time to leave the old ballasts, which are ideas of others and start our own, our mistakes, and our decisions.

Make your free time be your time, for you, when you learn to take time for yourself, then you will have time for everything else.

WHERE IS MY LIFE?
INSIDE

It is said that one day a woman was looking for a key on a street, a neighbor came and said, "what are your looking for?"; she replied "a key", and he started searching too, after 10 minutes, he said, "are you sure you lost it in this place", she then said, "No, of course not! I lost it in my house, but there is more light here than in there".

The annoyed neighbor said "crazy woman", then she told him, "Why do you call me crazy?" When you start looking for a solution to your problems, errors, defects, pain, you search outside for what is inside.

You fear discovering you murdered your inner child, realizing that you are becoming bitter and full of heaviness; the worst thing is that as a child you criticized that way of being.

So you wonder where your life is. You expect to find something outside of yourself, when you have it inside you since birth, it is in your senses, the 9 beautiful and tasty ways you have not had the adventure of living, because you limited yourself to 5 Aristotelian senses (taste, hearing, smell, touch and sight) and, sometimes, not even those.

You forgot you have the ability to feel another person's warmth (thermoception). You have the ability to know if something hurts (nocioception), to know when you are balanced (equilibroception) and to know your inner body (proprioception).

If you are not able to see the life around you is because you're doing something wrong; you are life and you are also death. And possibly, for being dead, your way is full of foul and unpleasant odor.

If you start to sow cute, beautiful and acceptable things for you, if you begin to accept yourself AS YOU ARE, then, the where and the inner being will fuse and do magical things and you'll begin to see the miracle.

Do not kill yourself and do not kill your environment, the emptiness you see around you is a reflection of what exists within you. Begin to believe and create. Be Reborn.

The Bible uses an interesting term: "metanoite" or "metanoia" which many have translated as "repent", but this is not so; that translation is very vulgar, we could say that "metanoia" is "to be born again". Being born again means to start over without doing the wrong things we did. That's where it changes. Within. Inside you.

WHY SHOULD I LIVE?

I should live because there is no better way to enjoy life. Because we have only one and we shouldn't wait for the waters to calm down to start surfing, the best waves for surfing come when the sea is rough, peace is perceptible as such in the middle of the storm. The best life is the one we fight for, the one we are torn for, the one that heals, the one that polishes and brightens our days and our smiles.

Live through the experience, amidst a world full of contrasts. Leave illusions and turn them into reality.

Live because you deserve to live. Live because nobody expects you to give your life meaning, living because it will hurt others and it's good to confront them to help them live.

No one will live your life as you will. Because you are your salt, your taste, your steps, your way, because you can share it with everyone, even with those you think you cannot share it with. With them you can see that your life is so full that everyone fits in it.

As you fit in ours, that's why you read us, that's why we communicate. Because life is that path that drives us to live together, without running, no winners, no competition, just living, believing and creating.

Marco Antonio Meza-Flores

HAPPINESS

WHAT DOES BEING HAPPY MEAN?

Usually we confuse happiness with joy; indeed, for some, it is a synonym. But joy is momentary therefore reactionary. Happiness does not depend on anything, it is a state of complete freedom, oblivious to the outside world, the environment and the circumstances, I mean, happiness is within you, it is a permanent state of life.

Being happy is accepting, walking despite the circumstances, falls, the troubles.

Being happy is learning to live in the present, enjoying what you have.

Being happy is deciding you want to be where you are or looking to be where your spirit feels free.

Being happy is getting caught up in what you want and not what they tell you to do; breaking that social contract which so many times prevents you from being you, why do you care about your reputation?, if this only cages you within walls and makes you bitter.

Being happy is to stop being a caged animal, remember that birds in captivity usually criticize the free birds because they do not understand what it is to be happy, they believe that happiness is the time in which they can spread their wings, of course, just inside the cage.

Being happy is accepting the challenge of life, enjoying your falls and your fears, learning that victories are not goals and mistakes are perspectives, opportunities to try again.

Being happy is to not stop trying, doing, seeking, believing, creating. Therefore we can say that being happy is to know how to live.

HOW TO BE HAPPY?
BY ACCEPTING YOU

One of the hardest things to do is accepting ourselves, we believe we do not deserve to be loved, to be touched, to be heard; often bombarded with very absurd ideas; "do not tell", "do not interrupt adult conversations", "do not express what you feel", "do not climb the tree", "do not do this or that", "do not study that or you'll starve to death", "do not follow your dreams or you will be a nobody", "study for a safer future", etcetera.

The media repeatedly states that we must be perfect in the eyes of others, the car, the mate, the job, the estate and the ideal body. The only thing that is not wrong in the word "Perfect".

Yes, we must be perfect, but the true perfection a human being can hope for is that in which he/she accepts their mistakes, walks with them, despite them and sometimes because of them. Only if they are accepted can they be used.

But beware, we do not mean that we should be happy with our mistakes; instead, we must accept that we have them to correct them.

In summary, in order to be happy, you must accept that you cannot change anything or anyone but yourself, and that you do not have the right to try to change others, only the obligation to change what YOU want from you, and not what others tell you that you must change.

WHEN DO I KNOW I'M HAPPY?

The answer is very simple.

Remember we talked about the senses earlier? Senses let us know, even the eyes smile when we are happy, the hands create, the mouth loves, heat expands and, overall, our body tells us.

We think the question was badly set, but it was necessary for the book because many people think this way. The real question, in any case, would be, Do you need to know when you're happy? The answer is no, happiness does not come from the definition of a word, happiness is a vivid and lived experience, a feeling, an emotion, meaning it has everything that makes me whole.

Being whole has to do with your senses, your environment, your angels and demons, your story, your dreams and nightmares, all of you. Just like happiness.

WHERE AM I HAPPY?

In our world, happiness is so coveted that one must be careful; most people are unaware that they are happy or do not know how to be happy, therefore, when they see someone who is genuinely happy, they immediately try to steal that happiness, believing that by doing so, happiness will transfer upon them. Nothing is farther from the truth.

Because happiness is an eternal state of mind, you must understand that there will be toxic people wherever you are, they may even be parents, siblings, friends, church, work, etcetera; and they will not want you to be happy, for they are miserable, and want you to be as well.

Now, let's not confuse being miserable with being evil; they are sick, injured, hurt, and therefore are miserable, unhappy, that is, without happiness.

So you must be happy in all places and in all circumstances, I do not mean you will not have problems, or that you won't feel bad when losing someone, but being happy is knowing how to enjoy even the disagreements of life, because nothing is final, except for happiness, why? Because others see you and that is the everlasting and lingering example.

Be happy everywhere, because happiness does not just get left at home or is it given to anyone, you cannot leave your happiness to the circumstances, people or things because it is within yourself and then can spread everywhere your presence touches.

WHY BE HAPPY?

Because there are so many things in the world that are offered to us and to be honest, they are not even necessary to live, much less to be happy.

The question seeks a cause to be happy, but happiness is the cause itself. After all, if you think about it, all natural pain as a result gives us a new life.

You have to be happy because it is the result of growing up, because it is the most humane thing that can exist, it is the most mature you can be and the most childishly you can play.

You have to be happy because it brings us closer to God and makes us one with Him; you have to be happy because if we are not, the pain will have been in vain.

PEACE

WHAT IS PEACE?

Peace has been confused with the absence of problems, evil, illnesses, arguments, etc., but that is not peace, peace goes beyond that and is attached to that, meaning, peace is to live with that reassurance that everything will be well despite all is wrong.

Everybody knows the definition of peace: That sense of control even in the midst of storms. And that's fine, we can live with it, but would you feel the same peace without those things that give us satisfaction, stability, joy, control?

That is peace, detachment of things, people, circumstances, everything, knowing you're naked, with nothing to protect you from what you are because you're not a name, much less a job, a title, a stereotype, you are not your things, your victories and your defeats, you're no son, or husband, or lover, or father. You are nothing and you are everything.

Peace is the complete acceptance that you don't need anything to live. Strangely, we have been told, and we believed, that we need something or someone to live, and this will give us peace, but when we live with such something or someone we want something else, and then torture comes to the picture and peace never arrives.

You are your own God, your own Buddha, and your own Christ, that's strange to some, because it would seem blasphemy; but if you think about it, these illuminists tell us about freedom, love, life, and especially peace.

Being ourselves we do not need what we've been told about religion, customs, our parents, our demons or angels, because we are peace and what is peace? It becomes a circle that has no beginning or end, because we are gods.

How to find peace?

Peace is not found, peace is in you. That's the problem, we are filled with so many things above, and we replace the peace we were born with, with superfluous things.

Imagine you are walking around your favorite place; you can be naked, do not carry anything that may obstruct you, behold your body and accept it. It is you in that body who perceives, who enjoys and one who hurts from the thorns in the path. Are you there yet? It is your place! Notice how all that is around you belongs to you; see the scenery you've set up, it is beautiful! Enjoy your place, your creation, contemplate it, love it, revel in it, there is no better place on the planet than the one you've created, because it's yours, that's where peace is, where you create it, wherever you feed it, that's what makes it fantastic, because it depends on you and what you put on and take off.

If you noticed I did not tell you about a beach or a valley, I did not ask you to imagine yourself in a prairie where birds sing and fly around you, I just asked you to imagine your favorite place, you did the rest, that's what peace is like, it puts you in places, it is up to you if they are pleasurable or war places. Do not imagine yourself with your loved ones or with superfluous things, you were naked, alone, but not in loneliness, that is, you were in the best company, yourself.

So, how do you find peace? Peace is not found, peace is activated, because it is part of your decisions, you cannot go around trying to find something that you already have, you just need to activate it, it already exists, but is possibly asleep. Wake her up! Awake yourself!

WHEN DOES PEACE BEGIN?
WHENEVER YOU WANT

Why wait until things settle down to activate peace? Why follow a stipulated protocol that says when "we can have" peace and when "we should be" overwhelmed?

Peace does not start, peace is. It is you who starts to live it when you're born to it, when you let go of those things that you laid on the road, that you tied your ankles to and which are now shackles that you do not want to drop.

Because these chains were fastened by yourself on yourself, they may have helped you, but now, once "matured", it is only your problem, like the camel which thinks it is tied just because they tied it with an imaginary rope, and if you want to take it, you have to crouch, and imaginarily untie it. That's the only way it will walk, dumbest thing you'll ever see, but it is real. The camel sits or walks depending on its imaginary rope. Good thing you're not a camel, just stop acting like one!

Peace is when you stop believing all the stupid things you were told and all the ones you get yourself into, that is, now you think that "having + doing = being". That is normal because we are governed by rules, which are as heavy as a tombstone on your back; however, peace teaches us that "being + doing = having" because it is my being who fulfills everything. Peace teaches us that, whether a have or have-not, one does not cease being or doing.

Now, if for some reason you think you are a camel, then go, untie yourself and start walking.

WHERE DOES PEACE BEGIN?

In a previous question we had already said that peace does not start, peace is.

Thinking that it starts somewhere is like saying that peace didn't exist until someone invented it, and peace was never invented, peace has always been.

Peace is not a product with which only the powerful and countries can trade. Fear is.

Yet despite the pain, the poverty of some, the excess of others, children sleep when the night arrives, because they have peace, they do not need a "tomorrow" or everything that it stores for him; a children's hope is not dead, they have not become senile, they have no expectation of tranquility, because they are quiet in themselves.

Be like children and let the days come and bring their own desire, when you accept them, you'll be right in the middle of peace.

WHY TO GIVE PEACE?
BECAUSE IT IS NECESSARY

Because peace is dormant in many people, giving it will possibly awaken it in them.

Peace is, but sometimes it is sleeping by the circumstances of life, the despair of others and selfishness of a few more. It is said that after the Second World War, a foundation gathered many orphans of all nationalities and fed them three meals a day; however, upon bedtime, children could not sleep, they cried, they hurt, suffered, and had difficulty to sleep. Some psychologists were called to figure the problem out. They analyzed the situation and after three days decided to give the orphans a piece of bread at bedtime. People did not know why, since the orphans had already had dinner, what was that piece of bread for? The psychologists said "they lost hope; without hope, peace is asleep, they cannot sleep because they do not know whether they will eat tomorrow or not. The piece of bread gives them hope, awakening peace in them, making them able to sleep".

Today at night, when you're about to sleep, embrace your peace or let it hug you; if you can't, run and take a piece of bread. When you wake up, share it with someone who wasn't able to rest their mind, their body and tell them "I share my peace with you!" by the way you treat them.

Marco Antonio Meza-Flores

ESSENCE

WHAT IS ESSENCE?

The question is profound because it contains several things; on one hand, the psyche, which is not a little ghost but the behavior that we have; also the soma, which is the body; and therefore, pneuma, the spirit. That is, the essence is your whole being, we are monist beings (we are one), not dualistic soul (behavior)-body and much less individuals[2], because that means "it cannot be divided into two". By being monistic, we are intrivitrios[3], which mean behavior-body-spirit, all in all.

In behavior-body dualism, good and evil fight each other, they are antagonistic, so one overcomes the other, in behavior-body-spirit monism, good and evil coexist and either one rules because it is fed more, but continues to live with the other, it accepts it as part of its being.

If you realize, we speak of "pneuma", which is the figure that many people are afraid of understanding.

---

[2] Literally means in-divi-duo that is "not to be divided into two."

[3] Intrivitrio means in-trivi-trio "that can not be cut in three." For those of Augustinian stance "soul, body, spirit"; otherwise see them organic, psychological and spiritual.

Jung would call it anima for men, animus for women. That is, we have to be comprehensive of our male and female sides, that makes us complete.

So the essence is that which is part of you and sometimes, without realizing it, you have built: your environment, your stories, your decisions, the name you accept, you.

HOW DO I KNOW WHAT MY ESSENCE IS?
WALKING

One of the biggest problems we face growing up is that identity questions begin.

Curiosity can be turned off and often exchanged for minor doubts. Hence we take our neighbor's smile, my parents' gestures, my friends' ideas and the clothes of the hottest star, all this to have "an identity."

You can see it in adolescents seeking identity, and that's not strange, it's part of the way, growth, part of oneself; the problem would be that an adult[4] should not do that, because it is assumed that he/she already has

---

[4] We stress that according to WHO adulthood is reached at age 29.

an identity. How many adolescents over 30 years old do you know? Are you an adolescent over 30 years old?

We don't mean this is bad, because these terms (good-bad) depend on our social environments, but we do believe that if you're still an adolescent after 30, you need help.

These days we hear messages that encourage us to live life dangerously: "Just Do it", "get rich or die trying", "you only live once (YOLO)".

The problem is not living life in a fun, daring or adventurous way; the problem lies in thinking that living should mean for us to be a copy of others, or being limited to the "fun/adventure" models taught by the media.

Along the way one should realize that one IS. No matter the nationality, social status, religion, routine, the profession; those are part of your being, but that is not you, that's what you've built with what you are.

Along the way you should see your essence, learn to walk with that feminine side we talked earlier (if you're male), cry, laugh, do the dishes and take care of the baby; or the masculine (if you're female), being tough, rude, or change a tire and burp amongst friends.

That's the fun of the way, not the club every weekend, the trip to the beach on vacation, Christmas gifts. It is not what you do but how you do it, what is the depth of your actions, how good you can become or how selfish and accept them both changing what prevents you to be better, you can be as you wish; rather, you'll be the one you decide, but in the way, always be you.

WHEN DO I KNOW THAT THIS IS MY ESSENCE?

If you wake up in the morning knowing that what you do on that day will give you peace, happiness and love; if you feel it completes you, you're on the right path towards and through your essence.

When you stop asking yourself where you are, where you're going and where you come from and if you know the answers to all those because you know yourself, you accept yourself, you admire yourself and you analyze yourself to grow, you're on the right path towards and through your essence.

When you stop seeing the bad things in life (which really do not exist) and feed what is good in it, you're on the right path towards and through your essence.

When you enjoy the day fully, without recesses, unequivocally, no taboos, no what-will-people-says, no nonsense social contracts, no pieces of paper that only serve as "airplanes" and are used to tell the curriculum you have, you're on the right path towards and through your essence.

Once you live a giving life. This we have heard many times, but it is truly a challenge. Think, when you give yourself, you will not have anything left but your essence and it will be, only then, when you have everything.

WHERE CAN I SHOW MY ESSENCE?
EVERYWHERE

You may have heard "We are all artists in what we do", but, so what? It is in you to define whether your art is good or bad. It is only in you, nobody else.

Octavio Paz said "human beings are people full of masks"; however, we believe that we can actually be original, without masks, we know it will be difficult, but not impossible, hence we have a unique essence.

Masks are routine, aren't you tired of doing the same thing even for fun? We are afraid to be different and show our essence because we may get expelled from the group, the family, from "my people".

Yes, your essence is you, but it doesn't mean you won't be toxic to others, that your behavior does not harm your environment, do not wilt the essence of others, because then yours is dying. Remember, he who seeks revenge or who does things in anger digs two graves.

The essence should be something pleasing to the senses of others. It is the perfume that creates a smile. It doesn't mean to seek the approval of others, No! Make no mistake, it is rather to live fully and that you like your essence, ask yourself, would you live with someone like you? If you respond positively then you're on track, if not, then start working.

Remember that your essence will be with you every day and everywhere.

WHY SHOULD I WORK IN MY ESSENCE?

Your essence depends on you, but you do not depend on your essence, remember we talked about "building the essence"? We will try to better explain it in the next paragraph.

Write your name down in the center of a blank sheet. Around it, write down everything you think you are professionally, emotionally, socially, culturally and religiously. You even are either a pedestrian or a driver.

Now read everything you think you are, analyze what you do not like, work on it. Working on your essence is necessary because you are unique. There is no one on planet earth or out of this world like you.

Sometimes we attach great importance to things we do not need, but not to those that help us grow, we have the great idea we are so alike to one another that we can't do better or different things because "they have always been done like this".

We also have the idea that everything is already done and we cannot do it ourselves.

Take a bucket, fill it with water, what do you see? Now shake it, what do you see? Let the waters calm down, what do you see? That is your essence, despite you are shaken, excited, in-love, mad and so on; your essence never disappears, it only changes form.

Why work on your essence? Because in the end and no matter how much the water is agitated, you must never allow it to become something that you were not willing to or do not want.

DREAMS

WHAT ARE DREAMS?

Dreams are an engine, a path and a goal. Remember what you wanted to be when you were a child, you then matured and came to adolescence and decided to be something else, then youth came along and you possibly disbelieved those silly dreams that would make you starve to death (your parents, teachers, spiritual leaders and possibly even friends warned you about that).

You came to "adulthood" or rather "came of age" and believed that "to be somebody" you had to seek accommodation in the economic and social construct. That you had to be part of the concrete jungle and that you had to put yourself somewhere to be "productive".

"Being a musician means you'll starve to death?" "How dare you want to be a writer?" "Be a philosopher? Come on! They never find a job!"

You have to be a lawyer, an engineer, a medical doctor, professions that give you money, so you can stop being poor, so that people say that "you are somebody in life".

Hence we think that dreams are an engine to continue, to not give up. Dreams are an engine to take the reins of your life and decide to go a certain route. How are you going to starve to death if what you love will feed you? How? If dreams are your engine and your way, the goal is within you, what you propose, in what you want and know you can achieve.

Calderon de la Barca said, "Dreams are dreams", Walt Disney said, "If you can dream it, you can do it", the young people on Mexico's Tlatelolco movement of 1968 said in their list of demands "be realistic and demand the impossible". All of them are those who urge us to believe and create, to go beyond the mental barriers that told us we could not achieve our dreams; only if you dream and go after those dreams will mental health be strong, mature and above all, human.

HOW DO I ACHIEVE MY DREAMS?
WALKING

Machado said: walker, your tracks are the road and nothing else; walker, there is no road, it is made by walking. The road is made by walking and looking back on it you see the road that will never be stepped on again. Walker, there is no road only wakes upon the sea.

We have a confession to make: there is no model, a manual, a guide, a step-by-step to help us achieve our desires. Therefore, we cannot tell you how to achieve your dreams; but we can tell you to see your footprint, the road is not what will be walked in the morning, it is what you've walked today. Then ask yourself, what you have walked, is it the way of your dreams? Dreams are not achieved, they are lived.

WHEN SHOULD I FIGHT FOR MY DREAMS?
ALL THE TIME

Even asleep, dream yourself, dream yourselves. What bothers us about the "reality" is that we believe that we don't have the power to change it. But reality is just another dream, a nightmare for some, but sometimes a nightmare is needed to wake up, because walking in your dreams means you're awake.

Being awake is to see your reality, to know you're a change agent in a sleeping society that limits you, that always says no to you. A society that calls you "crazy" and that will mock your dreams. We're not talking about taking a rifle, become a guerilla fighter and make a revolution against the sleepers; because if you did, you'd be more asleep than they are, blinded, lost. We talk about one step after another, to fight in the sense of peace that you know because you have already seen it.

The singer said: If I do not make a fried out of my enemy, why do I make war? If I do not fight for my dreams from my reality, why bother to wake up?

Morpheus tells Neo in "Matrix" he must understand that not everyone is ready to be unplugged and in fact, some are so immersed in the problem that they will defend the system to death.

You should also understand that yourself, when it comes to fighting for our dreams, we talk about doing it without stepping over anyone. Not to make war on others because they think or feel different than me, you should not force them to believe they are wrong. You must fight for your dreams yourself without making war on anyone, or anything.

Never stop fighting for what you want, at the end of the road you'll only have yourself and, if you believe in a deity, your creator; and you cannot fail either one.

WHERE DID I LEAVE MY DREAMS?

IN YOUR FEARS

The situation we live in "reality" leads us to not pursue our personal goals because we don't have the ability to do so. Accept the reality! This has always been told to us since adults believed we needed advice.

Another thing that is necessary is to accept fear. Many people have said for millennia that fear is part of you, part of your instincts, which serves as a defense mechanism, as a propellant and a bunch of nonsense and more nonsense, lies.

Fear is LEARNED, we're not born with it, it is taught to us, is not a defense mechanism, it is not instinctive, people do not have instincts, but drives, fear is not yours, you adopt it.

If adopted, it means that it is not yours. Why keep hosting it in your life?

Now, what to do with this fear? Face it, but before that, get to know it, accept it. Change sides with it. Make fear and everything it represents be afraid. You can't manage or dominate something you do not know. Something you don't know where it comes from, what causes it and in which part of the path did you decide to adopt it as your companion.

Unless you know it, accept it and turn your back to it, fear will be there at the side of your dreams.

We'll give you some instructions and then ask you to close this book.

Sit back, grab a notepad, on a blank sheet divided into two write down your fears, reduce them to 10, in the same way put your dreams, make them at least 10 and analyze them. Analyze where was it that you started to be afraid, think about why you don't have the courage to overcome it, and how you can do it.

On the other hand, fear is already there and your dreams too, if you realize, the list of dreams will be longer because you are more than your adopted fears, your fears are not you, your dreams are. They are part of your essence.

Beware and do not confuse dreams with having passive thoughts (PT) or stupid thoughts. Dreaming is to have something you can accomplish with your efforts, PT is to do nothing and wait for the miracle to happen, I mean, it is not wrong if you want to win the lottery, it is wrong not to buy the ticket. It is not wrong to want to be a star, an Oscar award winning actor, the next Pulitzer or Nobel Prize winner. What is bad is not to work for it. The problem is not to start acting for the Oscar, writing for the Nobel or the Pulitzer. That is PT.

Your dreams are where your faith in you is; if you are afraid, they will be refugees in there. If you dare you'll see them on your way, in your life, in your being. Nothing's wrong with wanting or believing and creating by thinking you are the best. What's wrong is not living as the best, not preparing as best, and not being able to take criticism as the best. Yes, it is likely that others will say you're conceited or arrogant, but it's not your fault they think so little of themselves. Then will you give your life to be the best every day? Life is every day, not a set of days that you turn to.

So dust yourself out, let your fears be disclosed, accept them and they will leave since they no longer have anyone to hurt; let your dreams breathe with you, let your dreams find you.

WHY DREAMING?

TO WAKE

We have heard many times that dreaming costs nothing, also, that it is useless to dream; so what do we have to lose? Every day we get up, to continue our way and our way is full of voices who complain people who are always complaining; even once you already complained.

But that who complains lives asleep in a reality imposed. Do you want to wake up?

Take a dream from the list you made, start to see how to do it, what you need, how long it will take to do it, how you have to start and start walking.

Dreaming is useless if it is not to awaken, to fight against yourself, against that that you are in this numbed situation you've imposed upon yourself. But you deserve it, because you live off it, you feed it, you depend on it and you will still decide your daily dose of reality until you understand that every story has an end but legends are forever, and they start with someone who dared to dream and made that dream a reality. After all dreaming is free, what costs and is worth it, is standing up to make those dreams eternal realities.

GOD

WHAT IS GOD?

This is such a complex question. God is, end of story. Trying to explain the unexplainable is so complex, talking about God is just babble for any human being. How can you talk about something which is not measurable or tangible?

Ok, you say that God is omniscient, omnipresent, omnipotent, etcetera. Attributes which have been given to God in the West in order to be able to talk about him, but they are still nothing more than babbling. God is not just that, God is more than that.

The philosophical game "God does not exist, He is" is real, because what exists is tangible, weighable and measurable; everything that exists has a beginning and end, God is eternal, therefore God doesn't exist, God is.

Throughout history we can find evidence of the attempt to describe God, but this is impossible for our small minds. We are not criticizing or diminishing this evidence, but, does any religion have a monopoly on God?

God is not a Christian, Buddhist, Muslim or Krishna, God is God, and He is so large that he fits in all religions and is there for any taste, so that you believe in him, even despite your lack of faith, because he even is with the atheists.

So, what is God? We do not know. We ran out of arguments, we don't have the slightest idea of what it is, but we can tell you that we walk with him/her every day, we cuddle, and sometimes we even fight, because God is so beautiful, that he cannot be described. You can only live in him, and that's where the wonder is. The wonder is the miracle of not seeing him, not defining him and still knowing that he/she is with you.

HOW DO I LOOK FOR GOD?
SHARING

A man went looking for God, but didn't find him. Sad for not having found him, he began to search for himself. He bought books, did meditation, but he could not find himself. Saddened, he said: "I'll look for my brother", and thanks to that he found all three.

When one begins to detach from the idealized "I", the "I" the society tells us we should be, that model of perfection harder to reach than God himself, and then one begins to realize the "We", the real "I". The "I" that is always with me and which was formed by what I want and which seeks to share. This is what we meant when we talked about awakening to your dreams, because waking up to your dreams is awakening, waking up to yourself means knowing that you are happy in everything, being happy is to have peace, having peace is to know that nothing is yours, detaching from all things. That's the cycle of life and life is in God, life is God.

Look for Him with all your being, but share what you know, what you have, what you are.

WHEN DOES GOD SPEAK TO ME?
ALWAYS, BUT YOU MUST BE STILL

God is everywhere, even where you do not want him to be. But be careful! Being still does not mean doing nothing, standing still is doing something.

Remember the story of David King of the Jews? He was not still, when all were at the battlefield and the king was supposed to go with them, he was in his quarters, pacing around his palace and that's very important. Pacing is going back and forth. He was looking through the windows of his palace, trying to find outside which could only be found within him, the true quiescence. Not only did his restlessness lead him to take a woman who was not his, who had an owner, but it also led him to plan the death of the woman's husband.

Everything you've done; all the distractions you have allowed, that harmful environment that makes you distracted, that makes you let the day pass you by without a single breath of life for you, that's NOISE.

Being still is to be attentive, gentle, willing, calm; ready to learn and listen. Not hearing, listening. Listening is an action that involves submitting your personal idea, your selfish desires to an understanding of the message from the humility of recognizing that we can learn from everything. That is to look for God and when one looks for God, God speaks.

When there is no noise, you can hear the voice of him who is on your side, you can listen to nature, you can hear the enemy, and then listen to God. But when there is no noise you can't appreciate the silence. You do not look for it or value it. Then surely through the noise is that you get silence. Learn to take the value off of noise, off anything that gives you false priorities, "self" meetings and remoteness from community.

You will hear the voice of God when you let noise do its job and you walk peacefully, when cheap distractors stop distracting you, when joy becomes secondary for its ephemerality and happiness becomes real.

You will hear the voice of God when you smile at his perfection as you see in the mirror. Even when you feel like he doesn't speak to you, ask yourself, what is causing noise in my head? Then, sit back, relax and stay still; you'll see that it is God.

WHERE CAN I FIND GOD?

IN EVERYTHING AND EVERYONE

That's interesting, usually human beings do not find God, but rather, it is God who finds them. In our life we walk, longing to be somewhere, feeling that, for once, the placidity of the finished work will last longer. We live like that, but we do not look for God. It is in that ecstasy, in that way that seems to lead nowhere where God meets us.

The problem is when prejudice will not let us see God in others.

We have been described an unattainable and wrathful God due to "sin", a God who moves away, a jealous God, but really, do you think God is like that? How will such an evil God give us the joy of life? How are you going to believe in a God who knows our nature, created it, and then rejects it? Ok, you may say to yourself: it is the original sin! That's a fallacy to control you, a prejudice to enslave you. That is the original sin. There is no such thing, it is an invention of San Augustine which to date continues to be believed, but do some research and you'll see it's a lie.

God seeks you in time and out of time, when you're up or down, when you think all is lost or recovered. God seeks you at all times. Do not confuse joy with happiness. Do not change the freedom to truly know God for the slavery of the institutional, wrongful and culpable god.

God's committed to you, he believes in your, otherwise, he would have created a different human being; so do not ask where God is, learn how to see him, here, now, in you. See God in everything and everyone.

WHY BELIEVE IN GOD?

Believe is a word that some do not understand. Believe is to trust, know and confess. Why believe in God? Because he is wonderful, not institutional as we already mentioned. He is the God of life, the God who accompanies you, who is inside you. That God who loves by nature, not the God who judges, think about this, why would God create something that he would condemn afterwards? Isn't it stupid to think of a God who says to you, I love you, but if you do not believe in me I'll send you to hell, or I love you, but ... if you are poor, homosexual, atheist, spiritual, different, and you do not believe what I, "the institution" tell you to, I'll send you to hell, I do not hate you but I murder you, I prosecute you and make you sick.

They asked a singer if he believed in God and he replied: I do not know if this god you speak to me about exists, but if he does, I think that he must be smart enough to not get mad by the question of whether this simple singer believes in him or not, and I think, if he truly exists, and he created everything we see, even ourselves, we are asking the wrong question. If I am his creation, am I worthy of being created? If he made me a human being, do I really know how to be human?

Believing in God represents learning through our journey that beyond price is the value of things and people. Believing in God means taking our rightful place on this earth, helping make it a better place, our space, freeing ourselves.

Believing in God means wanting to do more than existing, because some just exist, but at the time being, they do not shine.

Believing in God is the best satisfaction you will ever have, because that personal God of yours must be so great that in him/her there is room for everyone and everything. Think. If your God is not so wonderful as to give you the freedom to love those who are different and think different than you, get a different God and find one who likes to share and build a world for everyone.

RELIGION

WHAT IS RELIGION?

I think it's good to start from the etymology. Religion is a Latin word meaning "to bind tight, tie" real and figuratively. Do not confuse having a belief with having a religion; the first is the declaration of a belief in a deity, the second strictly follows a set of established ritual practice within a belief system or a set of ritualized practices, hence the dogmas and doctrines.

If we take the word from its root strictly, religion is "to tie something strongly," not only a God, it can be an object or a person.

Have you ever heard the phrase "he/she is their religion"? That's what it means, tie you to someone with a lot of psychological and emotional strength, therefore we can say that practicing a religion is to give that value to others. True religion, the one that's free of stereotypes and rules would be the one where you tie your mind, your effort and your time to do something positive in your environment.

It may also refer to an intention to collect or rebind the customs of the people with all new visions to institutionalize cultural traditions.

So religion also is everything that we want to bind to something or someone; religion is something that binds, that becomes institutional and has an expiration date. It is something that changes according to the criteria of the new education or technology. It is the union of an ideology or way of thinking with one's actions (Consistency), either based on faith in a higher being or the certainty that another human being has the ability to influence the fate of humanity.

We're not saying that religion is bad or good, the problem is not what to do but how to do with what we have at our disposal.

The Bible, Christianity's bedside book, predominant religion in the West, says that true religion is caring for the poor and orphans, that is, those who have less.

On the Buddhist side, Dalai Lama was asked what the true religion was, he replied: "The best religion is the one that brings you closer to God, to infinity. It is that which makes you better".

Then they asked, "What is it that makes me better?" He replied: "That which makes you more compassionate, more sensible, more detached, more

Marco Antonio Meza-Flores

loving, more caring, more responsible, more ethical ... The religion that you gets you to do that, is the best religion".

Then what is religion? It is what makes you a better person, a better human being and brings you closer to others, therefore closer to God.

HOW TO UNDERSTAND THE RELIGION?
LISTENING AND REASONING

A major problem is people confuse religion with spirituality, religion as mentioned above, is tie to you; and it is essential that people who want to be religious think about it, reason their convictions and contradictions.

Understanding religion is not rocket science; "commit ourselves to help the most vulnerable", simple, no problem, straight to the nitty-gritty, without so much bluster.

But, how can we understand the religion of others? Learning how to listen and search, every person is different, and religion makes us believe that we can understand God, and therefore its creation, but that's not true, each person sees God from a different perspective, that's why we have to "listen and reason".

A great danger religious people run is not listening to others because their God is not the same as theirs, and in doing so they close themselves to other voices, and when closed, they do not reason, it is their stomach (emotions) which guides them.

We reason because we need to understand things, not because we need to hide them, we reason because we need to make a judgment of situations, not because we point them out with the slightest iota of knowledge, and that is the problem to point them out, we take and copy the easy route, we do not read or study, we do not want to learn the view of others, the position of others, the way others see God. We just say it is flat out wrong, we copy arguments and thinking formulas of others; usually those who we believe the best, the leaders of institutionalized organizations.

Long story short, to understand religion we have to put ourselves in the place of others, not to judge, but to walk with him. Understanding does not mean justifying, it is learning from others.

There will come a time when only through love will religion have a real sense on the way, and there, we'll see that it is not a solitary one.

WHEN LEAVING RELIGION?
WHEN YOU GROW

Remember the words of John the Baptist: "it is necessary for me to wane for him to grow". He was talking about the Jewish Messiah. He firmly believed that the Messiah would deliver them from all evil, from all oppression and would give them freedom. He perfectly understood the work he had to do: to prepare, to make aware, soothe the ears of the foolish, proud and religious people.

John left his parents' religion, to take on a stronger commitment: Spirituality. He understood that it is not through a list of requirements set by the institutions that we can serve humanity/God, that we don't need to believe that we will die in a lake of fire to be better people, that God is not as warlike as to make you understand his love by sending you a disease to harm your body or who sends his fallen angel to tempt your heart and influence your decisions through fear.

He understood that there was something greater than his ideal ego: his life. Understood that what others say was their problem because they have to solve their fear and break the mental chains of years and years of fruitless, manipulative and questioning religion.

Leaving religion is the ability to detach from prejudice, leaving religion is to belong to a society that is above the set values, which makes you, learn from and love others despite everything.

You leave religion when you grow because growing makes you free, mature, responsible, and this is a freedom, a maturity and a responsibility free from attachments, fears and mostly free of prejudice and institutions.

If religion you profess doesn't help you grow, be free and give love, get away, you must grow, and what better way to grow than in moments of enlightenment and discovery about what is not convenient for me to live.

WHERE TO PRACTICE RELIGION?

IN YOU

If we believe those in need are those who are poor, orphans and widows, we could be disappointed. Need goes beyond material things. It is simple to deduce, but sometimes simple is anything but simple. Have you heard the phrase, there are people so poor that all they have is money? It is real. Some have the need to have money, money, money and forget important things of life, like self-loving, health, others.

Understanding that religion takes place in and with others, but that you can never give something that you do not have, meaning, if you do not have love for yourself, how can you love others? You do not respect yourself, how do you intend to respect others? You will never be able to give something that you do not have, simple to say, hard to live.

Love, forgive and redeem yourself. Accept your need and work on it. The best way to serve others is learning to serve you. Careful! It is not the modern phrase "me first, then me, and if there is time me again", it is not narcissistic, but it is a little selfish.

Being selfish is not something that hurts us, it is even healthy. It includes the ability to love, care, pamper, value, feel proud, applaud, question and analyze yourself. Wanting to be a better person for you, to understand the only competition you have is yourself and not others, to know that the center of MY WORLD is me, and that is healthy and beautiful, that's where I practice religion to myself.

Wanting to be the life center of others is narcissism and that hurts. Look at examples of life as Krishna, Buddha, Jesus, Muhammad, Gandhi, characters who before making the changes they made in their communities, worked on themselves. We don't say growth stops at a certain point, but you can share it when your needs are met.

Practice in you, and then you can give yourself in time and whole form.

WHY RELIGION AND NOT SPIRITUALITY?

The "good" religion is something social that needs others to be demonstrated, hence we should love the most vulnerable and needy, spirituality does not need other to be proven, for it is in oneself.

The "bad" religion needs a God and a devil for it to be strong, firm. It needs a war for the good one to win, while spirituality needs only one God to be happy.

Religion needs to see a distant, jealous God, who rewards your good deeds. Spirituality understands that God is in you, he loves you just as you are and your actions do not matter.

With religion you can be accompanied yet completely lonely. Have you ever felt that feeling where it seems you are surrounded by many people but you feel so alone? It is often like that with religion. Instead, in spirituality you are always alone, but never in loneliness, it's something beautiful and strange, spirituality is something that is shared, but you are alone, how is that possible? Simple, it is your responsibility to work your spirituality, for this reason you can NEVER be alone, you have you and by having you, you can't be alone.

Spirituality makes you arrogant in the opinion of the religious because you have the ability to understand that in this world everyone fits; but not in religion, there only those who believe and profess the same fit.

Spirituality is free while religion is usually oppressive.

SEX

WHAT IS SEX?

Sex from medicine is the gender distinction between two people, one that has a penis and one that has a vagina. However, we do not believe that this is the question we were asked. We believe that people are referring to genital sex between two people or more, depending on taste.

Sex refers to being in genital union with someone, but there are three ways to have sex for the psyche: making love, fooling around and fucking.

Making love: It is the commitment between two people who love each other and set goals for future growth as a couple, where they put on the table 9 senses plus their desires, goals, and dreams to be complemented as one but without losing individuality, it's a commitment of mutual enjoyment, but plans are made.

Fool around: It's like we say in Mexico "be someone's fuck-friend". There is a commitment but not as deep, the idea is to enjoy sex with the senses, but no future plans, dreams or goals are on the table, enjoy the moment and that's it. Here the commitment is mutual enjoyment, but without plans.

Fucking: It's to have where to empty my sexual needs, the idea of a prostitute or a gigolo fits here. I do not care if the other person enjoys it or not, I do and that's what matters. No commitment, no plans, nothing. It is completely satisfying for me only.

In America, the word SEX is so complex. It is full of taboos, because we fear it. We are not interested to mention it much less to do it.

If we go deep into it, sex is the pleasure found in stimulating any erogenous area. This could symbolize that cybersex and self-satisfaction fall within the restricted topic.

Sex as restricted issue is not due to a lack of information, it is society that restricts the subject to "good rules", it is not convenient for them that you would experience what it is to have pleasure in a determined way consciously, thoughtfully. Because if you have pleasure, you are free; and if you are free, you think; if you think, you'll know that what you do and how you do it deserves and involves care and responsibility.

Sex is the ultimate expression of responsible freedom, and the ultimate expression of pleasure.

HOW TO ENJOY SEX?

RESPONSIBLY

In the previous question, we concluded that sex is the ultimate expression of responsible freedom, and the ultimate expression of pleasure.

That means we should also understand that freedom is not an attitude distant from responsibility. In fact, at the time you accept to live in society the responsibility acquires the same value as freedom.

Sex is the same, one has the freedom to do it with anyone, anyhow and in the position you want, but responsibly.

You cannot enjoy something that will bring unpleasant or unwanted consequences due to lack of awareness, and that's what happens sometimes when one does not think how to enjoy.

Sometimes enjoyment is childish, i.e., pathological, sick, with tantrums. The thought is: "for me, regardless of others". This causes discomfort to the psyche, and what is around us, making enjoyment become a living nightmare.

Responsibly is not only the idea of using birth control methods, or taking responsibility for the consequences that not using them will bring, but a responsibility towards yourself and pleasure, it all depends on the kind of sex in which you are involved, whether you make love, fool around or fuck, you must do either one responsibly.

If you make love it is the responsibility of both to seek the pleasure of both, the enjoyment of both, the objective coexistence and building of things.

If you have fuck-friends, you will seek the enjoyment of both too, but you'll avoid engaging feelings that make either one fall in love, you should be aware of this, since it is hard not to get emotional when it comes to fuck-friends, due to subjective things floating in the air inside your relationship as friends. In any case, if the relationship takes you to "wanting to share your future with the person", that means you should take the step and stop fooling around with your friend and start making love.

Fucking, this case is very narcissistic, because you do not really care what the other person feels, it is just letting my desires, my anxiety, my sperm (if men) in one place, in one thing, and that's the vision of who fucks, the other person is merely an object to satisfy my desire for sex.

WHEN DOES SEX BECOME SELFISH?
ALWAYS

We had already mentioned that being selfish is not something that hurts us. It's even healthy because it includes the ability to love, care and value ourselves, etc.

So sex is selfish? Oh yes! Sex as any selfish thing invites us to be better people. While narcissism invites us to believe that no one can share my life with me because mine is the best, and no one can be like me, and I have the right to trample and annihilate the other because they are not like me.

Sex from the selfish point of view is not to seek personal satisfaction at all costs, but to share the satisfaction or pleasure with whomever you want.

If you're making love, you know perfectly well that is the pleasure with your life partner, the celebration party because you're together, so to speak. Having understood that while making love, the other is satisfied as you do and this makes you merge into one flesh.

If you're fooling around, you should know that the idea is just that. Both satisfy your desires, no compromise, no subjectivising, simply sex for the pleasure of having sex.

If you're fucking, your responsibility forces you to talk about this, as the commitment is with you, for sanity's sake you must make a contract between you and whomever you're fucking. It may be money, knowledge, companionship, etc., but it should be clear that you're just fucking, so no one gets hurt.

In all three forms of sex, selfishness is present, not in a perverse or pejorative way, but a mature and responsible manner.

Selfishness will lead us to understand that this is not about me, narcissistically, but about building a better world for me and to share it with another, in this case it would be in the area of sex.

Sometimes I ask some of my female patients to masturbate so that they explore themselves and know themselves, because many of them see it as dirty, bad or simply forbidden.

Men do not have the problem of masturbation, society does not see it "as bad" as in women, to them I ask to only see, touch and love themselves, without haste, without fear, because they were taught that it is only to stick it in, get it out without enjoying the process.

Why should sex be selfish? Because if we learn to love, respect and criticize ourselves, etc., we'll learn to give others what we have and that's our real self, openly, without fear and naked, what could be better?

Understand that even in sex, giving yourself is the most selfish act one can perform; but, before that, understand that selfishness is nothing wrong if love is present.

WHERE TO HAVE SEX?

Physically

Within the heterosexual area there are only 4 ways to have sex:

1. Penile-vaginal contact
2. Oral
3. Manual
4. Anal

In homosexuality there is:

1. Oral
2. Manual
3. Anal

Whether you're straight or gay, it is important to understand that pleasure is important for both, and we should be responsible for that.

Sometimes we hear that the man has or should have the freedom to put his penis into any vagina as he pleases, while the woman must be pure, but that is absurd, both can do with their genitals whatever they want, they are theirs.

Homosexuals are freer in this area, (for some people they are more promiscuous) and are also more responsible at the same time, the gay community made sure that people understand the need for protection, the need to care for each other, and that has worked for them so far.

Spatially

Wherever you want, like and feel like it. Without forgetting to take responsibility for what you do.

Psychologically

Imagination is one of the most important and exquisite instruments we have, knowing how to use it is beautiful. The imagination when you masturbate, when you do it with your partner, your friend or whoever, is VERY important, because it lets us create things and ways that we're not aware of.

The most important sex organ is the human mind. Every desire, pleasure and excitement all stems from there, imagination, then reach all erogenous zones and go back to the brain to send a message of enjoyment. This happens as the excitement or the action of having sex develop.

WHY TO HAVE SEX?

It is a physiological necessity for any adult as per Maslow, the psychologist, and his pyramid.

Your body is meant to be a temple. In temples there is silence and silence is pleasure and sex is when two bodies build silence in space it is achieved through a cosmic orgasm.

Regardless of social conventions, prejudices, taboos, everything that limits us and attacks our personal freedom, we are a full, unique, indivisible, beautiful and spiritual being.

Within this being, each of the primary, secondary or whatever needs, are part of the route we decided to walk and forge. Each adds a component that whole being we are, without it we are incomplete, and an incomplete being cannot give more than leftovers or crumbs.

More than a requirement, sex is an adventure. Do not have sex because it is a basic necessity, but because it is the building of your whole being, and that should be an adventure every day. A constant search for pleasure in you and that person you share your intimacy with.

We look for personal satisfaction: a good house, a good job, the pleasure stability gives you; sex is the same, looking for balance. The feeling of having what you need and enjoy it.

Hence, it is important to have sex, without it we are not complete, it is important to release energy and have endorphins, serotonin, oxytocin; neurotransmitters that give joy and invite to a constant state of happiness. Also, because it's delicious, is it not?

HUMAN

WHAT IS HUMAN?

A very complex question at this point in history, mankind has lost a lot of their "humanity". To be human ... be human ... human?

From the etymological point of view, human comes from the Latin Humanus, which is divided into humus meaning "earth" and the suffix anus which means "made of, derived from, taken from" speaks of the origin of something.

Considering this description, Human means "taken from the earth", "that which comes from the earth"; and this has to do with almost all cosmovisions of creation in the world, from Mesopotamia to the famous biblical Genesis creation.

These days man looks for stability that is increasingly artificial. We're no longer interested in the weather, if it rains we take an umbrella and simple, rain is good as long as we got into our car, the heat, we just feel that from our office to our transportation and from there to our home.

We have slowly stopped being "taken from the earth", to become "the earth's runaways", we have become rude, loud, dry, cold, intolerant, rigid as concrete. We're becoming more fearful of nature, forgetting that we are part of it; that somewhere in our being there is a piece of land on us, and each time that land becomes more eroded.

Being human is learning to walk in the rain, sun, cloud, wind, be a part of all elements that are in us, we are fire when we get angry and water when we cry, wind when we breathe and land when we create.

Being human is to see others as part of the land that we all are.

Being human is the consciousness of the three's thirst, the homeless animal, the ownerless, the ending forest, the fish without water, life going by.

To be human is to learn the value of things not for their worth but for what they mean.

We don't say it is not nice to have comforts, but to keep humanity among the comforts of life.

We're not saying it is bad to be rich, we mean do not forget those who did not have the same opportunities as you, do not stop giving to the needy and above all, never look down on anyone unless it is to reach out to lift them up.

To be human is to be yourself, learn from the fertility of the land, to embrace your inner fire, the spirit of thy wind, the life of your water. Complement yourself with the universe, i.e., understand that you come from the earth, understand its cycle, its course, become one with all.

HOW DO I LEARN TO BE HUMAN?
DIVESTING

The most complex thing we have inside our psyche or behavior is to divest or detach of things and situations.

Pain is inevitable, but being miserable is optional, this is real, we cannot put aside the pain you've felt for situations that have marked and left a scar on your life but, why don't you change the perspective? The scars can be "war wounds" and that means you "are alive", you survived, you learned where not to go, all that's learning potential.

Now you can help others going through the same thing, the idea is to let go in order to be free from the chains that bound you or you tied to your ankles. Think about how much time you've lost by trying to solve the past. Accept it and let it go.

We are taught to have, grow, own, build assets, family, people, friends, titles, etc.; we think that filling our inner, material warehouses will make us bigger, wiser, more recognized or at least happier ... accepted by others.

Diogenes of Sinope, the great cynic, teaches us to let go of that which makes us have need. He used to go to the market and laughed at all the things that were sold and he did not need.

Today we can see that the media tell us what we need, when we need it and why we need it, how many times have we heard some women say I have nothing to wear!

Letting go of things is so difficult because it involves the ability to decide that nothing or no one can stop your way to the land and on the land.

Divesting you of things means to just let them flow, knowing that everything will be fine. You flow, but sometimes you do not realize, or sometimes do not want to realize, because it is easier, and not frowned upon, pretending to hit a plateau.

You are a human being first and foremost, before your career, before your social role, your economic status, your tax obligations, you're a human, imagine it as such, delete your material things, your mental boundaries, what have you got? What's left?

If you analyze it, you have everything, but you learn to possess what you did not need until it became a necessity, but it is not part of you, because you have all you need since you are born, you are full of life, you're a winner, and still, in time you become senile, bitter, stupid, full of needs and empty and of humanity.

By speaking of victory we are not referring to the ephemeral things which are precisely the things that attachment defines to us as success: money, fame and fortune. Are you a human? Do you know how to be human? If your answer is yes, you have won. You succeeded; because it is for this that you were created.

Detachment is to stop being and do what is supposed to be done as per the social contract (and if you think about it, you didn't even sign that contract) and learn to do what you love to do: live, enjoy, give, love, forgive, walk, love, believe and create ... Ah, we wrote love twice because we believe this what a human being should know how to be best, love.

And we believe that through love we can let go of all the barriers that popped in my head.

WHEN DO I STOP BEING HUMAN?

When we accept the negative values, when we look for excuses for the situations we do, when we blame others for what we do, when we blame others for the reality we live in and in which we participate.

Being a human being, by itself, has no special feature, which makes you a human being is to have the ability to create; destroying is easy, any beast can do it, but to creating, that is Godlike.

In these times, people have stopped being with others, having face to face conversations, warm, beautiful, they just see and forget. Technological devices have nothing to do, because they are inanimate things, but we blame them because we do not take responsibility for our fear to share our life and people realizing the king of person I am.

One ceases to be human in the time we refuse to grow up, and that can happen very often, because comfort helps me feel safe, secure, non-threatened; but stop and consider, what is the cost here? In reality it is being always the same what you came to be? Are you not curious to see how far you can go?

You stop being human when you stop striving to achieve what you want, when you stop believing, creating, when you get into the comfort of saying "everything is good as it is, without changing anything in my being".

At the same time, you stop being human when you do not recognize yourself in others. When you do not see the great similarity you have regardless of race, country or gender; if you are more interested to relate to people who have the same things you do, titles, money, fame, fortune and power. If you are looking for identification by the way they dress, if they use the same brand of cell phone as you, if they despise people, if you've worn out for seeing the other doesn't have and see in you all you have achieved, then you've stopped growing.

Beware. We do not mean that you should not relate with people who encourage you to be better, to achieve your goals and dreams, to grow economically. NO! We want you to understand that a person, who helps you grow, will help you grow in all your areas, particularly in the internal ones, because if you're good on the inside, the outside is not so important, and no doubt, it will come at full hands. We have confused spirituality with poverty, and that's absurd. Equating material goods with economic and spiritual benefits that a human being can reach to grasp is equally absurd. Spirituality is neither in scarcity or abundance, it is in being. It is in being human.

You stop being human when you think "I'm like this, I'm not going to change, I do not want to change, why?" So learn to be human "I want to change, I'm going to change and I start to change."

WHERE DO I PRACTICE BEING HUMAN?
IN YOUR ENVIRONMENT

Let's remember what we said in the first question of this section, the meaning of human being "taken from the earth". Therefore, when you are responsible to your environment, from nature to those things that man has created, you're a being a human being.

We don't mean you should despise those things which have been irresponsible with the environment, we mean do not be destructive. The most logical about nature is giving, to continue the cycle of life; be like nature.

The praxis of being human is complicated, especially in such a noisy world, full of "good, well-meaning people", what do we mean by this. Sometimes wanting to be human becomes so complicated because, as much as one wants it, it seems that the attitudes of others do not deserve it.

But that's a lie. The attitudes of others do not matter if you do not give the required value. The problem is not being selfish, the problem is being mean; as that who gives ten because he can spare them and also looks for ways to make a hundred.

The goal is to receive only as necessary. So many people fought with their faith and prefer to save at the expense of others, before you venture to trust that it all will be given.

In charity we can also practice being human, but it is not the "Oh you need me, I will save you!" charity, but a charity to let go of things.

In love we practice to be human beings, because it is the ultimate expression of dispossession and charity toward others; therefore, it is the ultimate expression of humanity.

At home I can practice being human, when I am with my loved ones, and I can hear them, listening to them is an act of love, not passive, it is an action so it forces me to do.

At work I can practice being human, when I walk with that employment, position or company partner and I practice believing and creating, loving and giving, learning from them.

Anyways, in every activity that you develop, in every idea you want to create, in the way you treat others; whether family, friends or colleagues; remember that before any position you are still like them: a human being. Harmonize! Love! Give peace! And everything will flow and you'll be Human.

WHY BE HUMAN?

In our social environment, being subversive is a risk and is frowned upon. Loving, making peace, being free and human is subversive and that is not good for our current society, because for it is best to "oppress, hate, have resentment, enslave", the idea is robotize your mind. You can see in every social institution, schools tell you how to study and what is best for you, churches tell you what you have to believe and how you should worship, communities that show you what you shouldn't do and how to do things, but few, very few that teach you to think for yourself, to create for yourself, to stumble and still continue despite the setbacks.

We're asked why to be humans. Just for the sake of proving to yourself that life is full of projects you can do in your mind, because it only takes one to start changing the social environment.

Marco Antonio Meza-Flores

It is said that in a Japanese community there was a small village among all others that was surrounded by mountains, rarely did the sun shine upon it, people grew very weak and therefore fragile, then one day an old man said, "I will remove the mountain, I'm tired of the sun not sharing its strength with us", and the young men said, laughing, "how shall you remove the mountain?" "Only with this spoon!" replied the old man, they laughed and asked "do you think you can remove it?" The old man replied, "I do not know, but someone has to start!"

That's the idea: for someone to start being human, someone to dare and say "Enough! I want to be what I should be" someone who wants to put aside the social contract and takes the risk of living ethically and not in popular morality.

Being human because that is your purpose in this life, that's what you're made for.

If you see a cat, its whole life will unfold as a cat, it will eat like a cat, it will procreate as cat, will purr like a cat, the cat knows its role in life! ... Do you know yours?

Look at society, look at the general picture from outside and observe the roles performed by different people; if you look a little more, you can even see their attitudes, motivations and purposes. Now go to the mirror and see yourself, do you like what you see?

What's your role in your environment? Would you like to live with someone like you? Do you like what you do, what you want, what you've become? How does what you do affect your environment? Do you create or destroy?

If you answered no, no, no! Do not worry! Go to the kitchen drawer, pull out a spoon and begin removing the mountain.

If it was yes, the road will be long, winding, and even prickly, but in the end, the arrival will be beautiful ... keep going, being human is closer every day.

Marco Antonio Meza-Flores

FAMILY

WHAT IS FAMILY?

Etymologically speaking family has two connotations. The first one comes from the Latin famulus which means "servant or slave." The other description could come from famel, from the root fames (hunger) could be said this way: "core which covers all my needs" or "group of people who eat together in a house".

But in today's society, what is family? For some, families can be described in many ways. Some see nuclear families which are the foundation of society (institutionally) and depend on the father, mother and children. However, there are extended families, where people who are akin live together, uncles, cousins, grandparents. There is also the single-parent family, where there is only one figure in the role of "parent" and there are "other types of families" that can include friends, or siblings living together.

For us the family has something of both etymological roots. You can either become a slave, or it can be a group that meets all your needs, economic, psychological, social, cultural, ALL OF THEM.

In order to define what family is, we could start by saying what it is not.

Family is not one that limits your dreams, your faith in yourself, your ability to create for yourself.

Family is not that which stops your physical, spiritual or intellectual development, limiting you to what they want you to be.

Family is not the one which takes care of you because they believe it is their duty.

Family is not to meet the whims of members because "it is your duty as the subject of it."

In short, family is that group of people, with your blood or not, who become your mother, your father, your brother, your sister, husband, wife, son, daughter, uncle, aunt, grandfather, grandmother; people who are responsible for teaching you and learning from you, people who live and coexist with you throughout life.

The family is the social unit that begins with you, when you give yourself, when you love enough to give yourself and you're willing to be loved.

Family is pleasure, love, security, believing and creating; it is learning to love to give you, beginning a path where everyone arrives together, because everyone's going. Where a better world is built, a world where everyone fits.

HOW DO I IDENTIFY MY FAMILY?
LOVING

We have said that loving is giving you, and love is precisely the formula for all, and what could be better than loving everyone; family will be those who connect with that love.

When you love, you reveal the fear in others, even your own fear to be loved, and to love in the same way. That's why the feeling of being part of a group of people is very difficult, and sometimes we seek to avoid it, but this is a very immature attitude. Just think how many adolescents adopt the loner pose, "I make myself worthy" or "nobody tells me what to do"; because that is an irresponsible attitude, it is not about obeying or not, it is about working together to achieve a desired goal.

At the time you find someone who shares your pathologies, your craziness, your demons, your fears, but at the same time shares your dreams, daydreams, fantasies, goals, utopias, feelings, loneliness, and then you can, if you want, make them family.

50 ANSWERS

Your family is one that sees you as an equal, regardless of the family role you perform in the group.

When you find someone who you are able to give yourself for, push yourself and demand them to be better, someone who you want to keep a unit with, not forgetting the differences but coming to love them, accepting them and living with them, through confrontation in love when they are wrong. Remember: The idea is to grow.

Now, be careful, love is not simple. It hurts. Along the road you're going to find people who want to take advantage of your love, people who will pretend to be a part of your chosen family.

But love is not only pain, on the contrary, love is satisfaction; we don't mean that you should like pain, but that you should understand that, as pleasure is, pain is part of you and you should accept it as such. What a kind of life would this be if love is just enjoyment, everything in just one side is boring, so you need to play in the pendulum's movement. If the pendulum is static, it is dead; if it stays on one side it dies, if it moves, lives.

Even your blood family may be the ones hurting or using you; however, it is up to you to keep inviting them for coffee.

Then, when you want to identify your family, look inside yourself, not in social standards, or what is "politically correct" and also look inside them, when you fill the needs of others, your being will be overflowing, when your being overflows, then you can share with others.

WHEN SHOULD I LEAVE MY FAMILY?
WHEN YOU MATURE

One of the things that humans find the hardest to do is detaching from family, indeed we are mammal which takes the most to separate from the core.

Obviously it is assumed that human beings are social intrivitrios, as they grow, they integrate into a particular role.

During growth, it is understood to be the family that lays the foundations of values and attitudes as well as the tastes and preferences that will serve as a starting point to adhere to their environment.

When one matures, one must leave the family. Read again, YOU MUST DO IT. This could sound harsh or cold but it is important to know that when you grow up, you need to create your own family.

If your biological family does not help you grow, walk, believe and create, it's time for you to leave. We have heard many times that it is not good to separate from those who carry our same blood; but in no way is it healthy to eat in a harmful environment for your being.

It is not to stop loving them, but do not coexist with them if they are harmful. It is about setting boundaries that make you and they grow, without being forced to put up barriers to not see each other ever again.

Each and every one of us gets tired of an environment where there is always suffering, sorrow, pain, blame, pointing fingers, etc.

It is therefore important to mature, learning to see your loved ones with the best objectivity, knowing that they are not perfect. Neither are you.

Leaving the family is healthy, mature and, above all, is part of a path that will make you create and believe in your own family, in your purpose.

WHERE TO STAY AS A FAMILY?

HOME

As we mentioned, families are formed. However, we know that one with the same blood is not chosen, but the family which is the "core that covers all my needs" can be chosen, that is the great thing about knowing how to be and how to make a family.

Life often becomes a constant swing of emotions and feelings. This normally makes wounds and scars in us. Family, the real family; one that you've forged over the years and you have attached yourself to, is good for those moments where the pain is closing in, because it cures, heals, anoints with the balm of love and true.

Triumph is enjoyed as a family. Defeat must also be lived as a family because family is what encourages us to keep going.

And it is not kilometers or miles, we can be on different continents, but you know who your family is.

Hence the word home, comes from the Latin focus, which is where fire comes from in Spanish, the symbolism comes from Rome, when they used to always have "lit fire" at home, for the presence of the gods to be in the house. If the fire was missing it meant it was a house with no gods and therefore without faith, without shelter, without purpose.

Home is to keep the fire of family lit, it is not a place, it's a lifestyle, you take home with you; it is built with everyone.

Home is the attitude to fight, defend, prevail and push the flame of family forward. Belonging to a family is to have a home and having a home is to keep the fire. Fire is hope, desire to create. The faith that keeps us together, that makes us family.

WHY CULTIVATING A FAMILY?

TO HEAL AND SAVE

It is difficult to grow, as the years pass, we attack, damage, hurt, lacerate, seek revenge, competition, a podium from where others can see us.

We are also recipients of betrayals, lies, blackmail and gradually, our relations, those bonds, those extensions of ourselves erode completely, sometimes due to cause and effect, abandoned.

Have you ever felt this way? Have you caused that? How many times have you been through similar situations, stayed silent and let it pass and let someone else within "the family" do that?

And as we said due to "cause and effect" they got it wrong.

However, family must reconcile. The best sign of a healthy family is not one that has no problems, but one that solves them as a whole, as a unit, as a body.

Reconciling comes from Latin reconciliare, which means "bringing someone back to the meeting, assembly, council", that is, restore union, bringing back that who is gone, reach agreement with that who we have separated from.

That's the interesting thing about the Jesus from the Bible, he sends his 70 followers (not just the twelve apostles) to go to the cities to be reconciled to God, his idea is that, the man who has been separated from God reconciles with him, because he is part of the family. Because their faith is their home, their fire; in the end, it is the hope in this unit and certainty of what we can achieve, what keeps us as a family.

All loneliness, all rancor, each of the situations that have separated us from our family must be restored, because that is healing, by restoring then we save our family from loneliness, hatred, and other pathologies or demons.

It is not sailing with flag of impunity, saint or wise. Rather, recognize in oneself the evil of others. Turn to see our own faults, our own emptiness. Heal and fill ourselves with what we want to be the common denominator of our family.

Family reconciles, and if it is you who needs to turn to the unit, do it.

CONTENTS

HUMAN

FAMILY

CONTENTS